Brunei's Bespoke Rolls-Royces
Unlimited Money, Automotive Passi[on]

By Richard Vaughan
First Edition
ISBN 978-1-387-69458-7

©2018 363Insights LLC

Accuracy is important. Every effort has been made to provide credit for the numerous pictures contained in this document, but some images have unknown sources. If you deserve credit for an image or if you would like to provide corrections or amplifications, please contact:

Richard Vaughan
363insights@gmail.com

CONTENTS

The Bespoke Motorcars of the Brunei Royal Family	5
SZ Series Estates	9
Silver Spur Limousines	19
B2 and B3	21
Buccaneer	31
Continental R Four-Door and Limousines	39
Continental R Sports Estate	45
Continental R Super Short and SWB	53
Dominator	57
Grand Prix 190	63
Grand Tourer Imperial	67
Grand Tourer Monte Carlo	71
Highlander	75
Bentley Java	83
Pegasus	93
Majestic	101
Royale	107
Phantom V	113
Phoenix	117
Bentley Rapier	121
Cloudesque	125
Silverstone	129
Spectre	133
Statesman	137

*THE BESPOKE MOTORCARS OF THE
BRUNEI ROYAL FAMILY*

Few publications have gone into any great detail about the secretive collection of coachbuilt Rolls-Royce motorcars and Bentleys commissioned by Sultan Hassanal Bolkiah and his brother, Prince Jeffri, of Brunei. The Sultan, often described as the world's richest man in the 1990s, has become a living legend for being the one person who has lived the dream that all enthusiasts have; having the wherewithal to turn his dreams into reality, be it with cars, planes, or homes. More importantly, besides having the money to achieve his automotive dreams, he controlled all of the laws and vehicle regulations in his country. This meant that he didn't have to comply with the pesky regulations and safety laws that effectively ended the coachbuilding business elsewhere in the world, even for the ultra-rich.

Thanks to a 50% share of Brunei's oil revenues and to shrewd investments around the world, including some of the most famous real estate parcels on earth, The Sultan's income was estimated to be in the range of four to five billion dollars per year at the time that he was so heavily involved in creating his dream cars.

At one time, he was known in the media as a free-spending playboy, but in the late 90's, he began to take his role as ruler more seriously. In order to underpin his absolute monarchy, he began reinforcing more conservative Islamic values. It is said that all of the free-spending presented an image problem for Prince Jeffri, who owned a sixty meter yacht rather indelicately named, Tits, on which he was rumored to have held wild parties at which almost anything was possible.

Ultimately, The Sultan's new conservatism forced Prince Jeffri, then Brunei's finance minister, to stop spending on cars, planes and parties. However, before the fun ended, The Sultan and Prince Jeffri had hundreds of bespoke motorcars made-to-order.

When he first started with coachbuilt commissions he quickly discovered that most of the cost was in design, engineering and development, not in building. As a result, the cost of making large numbers of cars wasn't much higher than making one. They were almost always made in batches of 6, 12 or 18.

At one point in the mid to late 90's, an entire coachbuilding industry was humming along in both the US and in Europe in support of the car collecting hobby of these two gentlemen. The treasure trove of 3000 cars has been estimated to be worth up to 8 billion dollars. Of course, that's purely speculative because no one has really seen the cars and most certainly it is true that they have never been counted and catalogued by anyone outside of the Royal garages.

The hoard is made up of mostly high performance exotica and ultra-luxury formal sedans and limousines. In this collection, the extraordinary is ordinary. The Brunei Royals ordered thousands of cars from a variety of manufactures, not just from Crewe. There are no less than eight McLaren F1s, hundreds of Bentleys and Rolls-Royces, Ferraris, and Aston Martins. On top of that, there are said to be thousands of more ordinary Mercedes and Porsche automobiles.

There are, of course, hundreds, if not thousands of people who know intimate details about the royal collection, but they have all signed extensive confidentiality agreements. Those individuals worked in various capacities on the cars in such jobs as design, engineering, testing, validation, etc. Beyond that, there was an extensive service staff to take care of the secretive royal garages and the all of the cars inside of them. Reportedly, many of cars are stored in garages by color rather than by make.
Many of these cars wear colors that would be considered startling to western eyes, but would be considered fabulous in many other parts of the world, particularly the Middle East and other Islamic countries. These colors include mint green exteriors matched with mint green interiors and bright yellow cars with bright red interiors. Reportedly, each family member had a favorite color combination and all of that person's cars were ordered that way.

Being a professional car designer, I have known numerous people who were involved in either the design or engineering development of the Sultan's Rolls-Royce and Bentley collection. I did design work on a Brunei Ferrari myself. As a result, I have been able to gather some interesting information and a few unique pictures of the cars. Some of the images on these pages have come from contacts in the industry. Many of the other pictures are now in the public domain, having been published hundreds of times on innumerable websites without attribution.

One of the most interesting facts that I learned is that for some of the cars that were made in small batches, the body panels were stamped on tooling rather than being hand-beaten as you might have expected. This meant that the cars were of unusually high quality. One person I spoke who owns a well-known automobile engineering firm said that they were absolutely the finest cars to have ever been built in small numbers.

Also of note is the fact that Rolls-Royce developed a special engine specification for the Sultan's cars. Known as the "Sultan Spec Engine", "Sufacon" or "Blackpool Engine," it powered many of his Crewe cars.

The cars were designed and engineered by a number of specialty automotive design houses around the world, many of which are only known to people working in the car industry. However, they were constructed at some of the most well-known design facilities in existence such as Pininfarina (Italy), McLaren (UK), Metalcrafters (USA), ASC (USA) and at Dauer (Germany).

Interestingly, because the cars were ordered through Rolls-Royce Motor Cars, the chassis numbers have been recorded with the UK government and a huge number of the cars were first registered at the various UK homes of the Sultan and as a result received UK registration numbers, meaning that we now know the names of some of the cars even if we don't know all of the details about them.

Over the years, enthusiasts have managed to photograph many of the cars in both the UK and abroad as they were being used as transportation. Some of the most interesting pictures are actually just pictures taken of the royal family alighting from the vehicles. In many of those pictures, a quick look beyond the subject matter reveals the amazing motorcars that they arrived in. Furthermore, over the years, many of the cars have been sold off and have appeared in various publications for sale.

The following is the most comprehensive collection of images that I have been able to put together of the various Rolls-Royce and Bentley motorcars owned by the Brunei royals. Not included in this book are the ten Continental R convertibles ordered in 1993 and 1994, which later was sold by the company as a regular production model called Azure. They were indeed bespoke motorcars, but to the enthusiast's eye today, they appear to be standard Azures.

Some of the pictures in this book are of very low resolution. Many are of poor composition and quality due to the fact that they were almost always taken surreptitiously by somebody who probably should not have had a camera with them.

All Rolls-Royce and Bentley motorcars built for the Royal Family of Brunei used this tread plate.

It is most interesting to see that even though the Continental R-based motorcars for the Brunei royals were supposedly top-secret, they often had brochures of their own or were shown in rather standard brochures without notice by the public. In this case, the B2 and B3 coupes, the four-door Continental R, and Silverstone were revealed in small images in the back of a rather rare, but standard brochure that celebrated the end of the production of the Continental R and Azure.

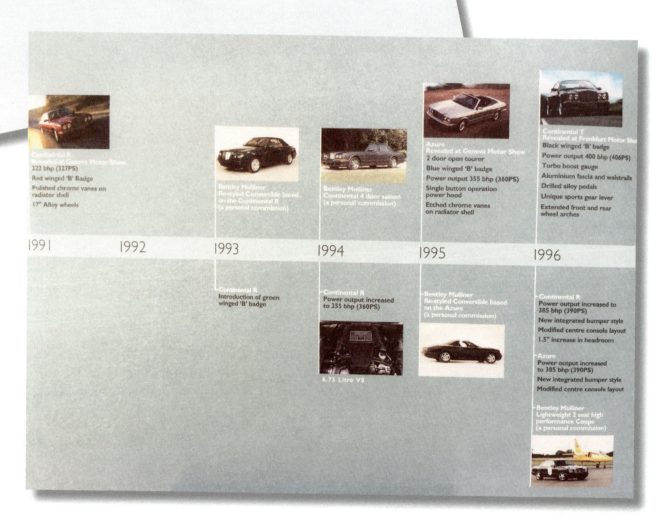

SZ-SERIES ESTATES

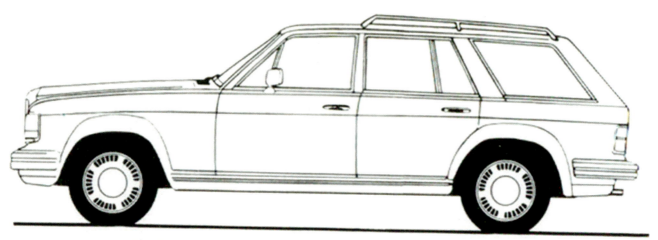

Val d'Isere

Far ahead of its time was Jankel's fabulous four-wheel-drive estate model, the Val D'Isere. Its four wheel drive system had its front wheels driven hydraulically by motors built into the modified front hub assemblies. They would only be engaged by selecting low or reverse gear and the front wheels would automatically disengage at speeds over 30 mph.

These wagons were favorites of the Brunei royals, but other enthusiast bought them as well.

Undeniably practical, these conversions by Jankel almost never come up for sale.

There is no doubt that it looks extraordinarily smart on the more modern, wider Continental T wheels and with vented front wings. These images were used for advertising when the car was for a sale in the early 2000s.

Val d'Isere

The Val d'Isere is an elegant but practical estate conversion, based on long- or short-wheelbase Rolls-Royce and Bentley motor cars.

During conversion, the rear of the motor car is shortened and coachbuilt into an estate vehicle configuration.

Robert Jankel Design's own four-wheel-drive system is optional on all Rolls-Royce and Bentley conversions. It was developed originally for the Val d'Isere, to provide drive to all four wheels at low speeds. The rear wheels are conventionally driven through the motor car's normal engine and transmission system. However, the front wheels are driven hydraulically by motors which are built into each modified front hub assembly. The motors are powered by an hydraulic pump which is connected to the transmission via a toothed belt-drive system.

Drive to the front wheels is engaged by selecting low or reverse gears, disengaging automatically when the motor car's speed exceeds 30 mph.

This snippet from the Jankel Val d'Isere brochure describes the mechanics behind the four-wheel drive system.

The woodwork was truly stunning, with rounded door caps inlaid with contrasting veneer.

As with the Silver Shadow conversions, the Crewe suspension design forced a rather limited cargo capacity on the engineers.

Photos both pages: Chelsea Workshop London

This well-known and somewhat extroverted example was reportedly ordered for the Brunei royal family. A number of Brunei cars were ordered in this bold color combination.

A 1:43 version is quite rare and is a must-have for collectors.

Looking rather restrained in dark blue, this example is often seen being used as regular transportation.

It is interesting to see one in pearlescent white. While this is a somewhat common paint nowadays, it would have been very special when this car was new.

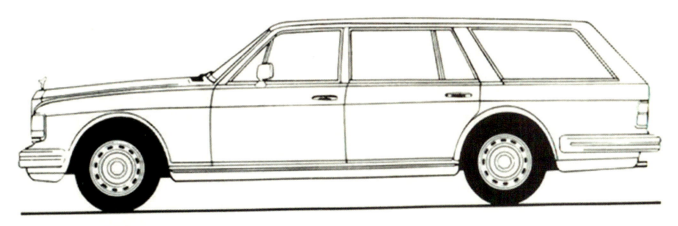

Provence

The Jankel Provence was similar to the Val D'Isere, but presented on the long wheelbase chassis and with a longer rear overhang. It is unclear how many were produced, but they are almost never seen.

SILVER SPUR LIMOUSINES

The Brunei royals have a number of ceremonial limousines on the SZ chassis in both Rolls-Royce and Bentley configurations. They range in presentation from conservative to ornamental, such as the ones seen here.

Here, the Sultan's fifth daughter, Princess Hajah Hafizah Sururul Bolkiah, rides to her wedding. You can see that not only is the car decorated with highly ornamental wedding trim, but the sheet metal of the car also differs from that of a normal Silver Spur limousine. Note the body lines toward the rear.

BENTLEY B2 AND B3

Paolo Garella has generously talked about his experiences at Pininfarina where many of the Brunei cars were designed and built. At that time, Mr. Garella managed the Pininfarina Prototype Engineering and Manufacturing Department. Later in his career, Andrea Pininfarina gave him the prestigious and important assignment of leading Pininfarina Special Projects, the division of the company established to exclusively handle bespoke builds, a position he held for seven years. In both roles, he dealt with not just the design, engineering, and manufacturing of fabulously extravagant coachbuilt cars, he also had to deal with the often colorful personalities of their owners.

Fortunately, he has gone into detail about those projects for the benefit of car enthusiasts around the world and has stated publically that both the Bentley B2 and B3 were based on the Continental R and that 13 of each were built. Until he confirmed this, we were only able to speculate. The B3 was the second project, but was the first to be delivered.

According to Mr. Garella, they were the first completely bespoke Bentleys for the Royal Family of Brunei and it was specified that the first of the cars would be delivered for the birthday of Prince Jeffri. The first of the cars was shipped on a special plane and arrived in Brunei on the night of the party where it was to be presented. According to Mr. Garella, the humidity levels were so high in Brunei that that the cars were wet from sitting in the ambient air and many of the electronic features were non-functional at the presentation. Mr. Garella has told an entertaining story about how, on the day of the big reveal, he received a phone call saying that the steering wheel was not installed straight. As a result, he and his crew rushed to the site of the pending unveiling of the car to begin fixing the problem. Just as they had removed the steering wheel, the royals and their courtesans walked in to see the car. Apparently, they were exceedingly angry at the unfinished state of the car as such a critical moment. After all was made right, the car was a viewed as a great success. The only change was that the interior of the B3 was preferred, so that interior was retrofitted to the display car and was installed on all of the later cars.

The yellow car is an example of the B3. The green car is a B2. They are similar, but clearly quite different.

Two of the three images on page 174 are of the Bentley B2 in Pininfarina's photography showroom.

Seventeen B2 cars were made between 1994 and 1996 with the following chassis numbers:

Model year 1994

- SCBZB04C5RCH52042
- SCBZB04C4RCH52131
- SCBZB04C2RCH52161

Model year 1995

- SCBZB04CXSCH52351
- SCBZB04C1SCH52383
- SCBZB04C2SCH52389
- SCBZB04C8SCH52431
- SCBZB04C3SCH52434
- SCBZB03C3SCH52435
- SCBZB04C7SCH52436
- SCBZB04C2SCH52442
- SCBZB04C4SCH52443
- SCBZB04C6SCH52444

Model year 1996

- SCBZB16C9TCH53169
- SCBZB16C4TCH53175
- SCBZB16C8TCH53180
- *SCBZB16C5TCH53184*

Twelve examples of the B3 were made between 1994 and 1995. All 12 chassis numbers are known.

Model year 1994

- SCBZB04C7RCH52074
- SCBZB04C4RCH52081

Model year 1995

- SCBZB04CXSCH52334
- SCBZB04C5SCH52368
- SCBZB04C8SCH52378
- SCBZB04CXSCH52382
- SCBZB04C7SCH52386
- SCBZB04C0SCH52391
- SCBZB04C9SCH52437
- SCBZB04C0SCH52438
- SCBZB04C2SCH52439
- SCBZB04C9SCH52440

Bold color choices were made for both the exterior paint and interior leather and colors were combined that were seen as unusual pairings to Western eyes, yet seem quite appropriate in other markets. The design of the rear compartment appears to be particularly cozy and elegant, even in an unfinished state, as seen above.

They are not the best pictures, but at least they reveal that this is B3 number 11.

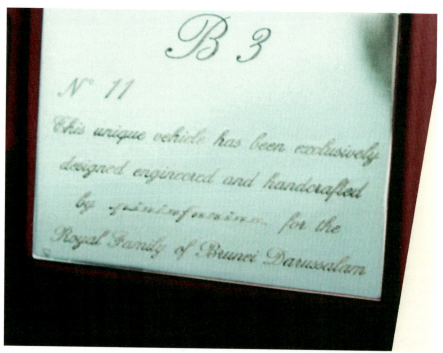

An incredibly elegant car from any angle, it's a shame that the car enthusiast community was not able to enjoy seeing them on the road.

The two images above, left, are of the B3. The two on the right are of the B2.

This rare image is of the B3 outside of Pininfarina's offices.

BENTLEY BUCCANEER

The Buccaneer was a two-door 2+2 coupe designed in a style reminiscent of French coachbuilding of the pre-war era. There were six examples of this fabulous looking design.

Both the exterior and interior were designed by GMD in Coventry, England. Styling work started in October 1994 and was finished July 1995. It was known as project P550.

This appears to be the model that is most beloved by the Brunei Royals based on the fact that they are frequently seen and there are reports of them being the recipients of regular maintenance.

The chassis numbers are:

- SCBZH16C3TCH00434
- SCBZH16CSTCH00435
- SCBZH16C7TCH00436
- SCBZH16C9TCH00437
- SCBZH16COTCH00438
- SCBZH16C2TCH00439

This car possesses one of the most dramatic designs of any Bentley of the post-war era. No detail was left untouched by the designer's hand. Every exterior surface and every interior surface worked to create a cohesive and fully integrated design.

Six copies of the Bentley Buccaneer were built for the Royal Family of Brunei Darussalam. They were built by Heuliez, the famous French coachbuilder, in 1996, on what was known inside Crewe as the ZH chassis. Each has driver and passenger airbags and it is said that each one was fitted with the "Sultan spec" Blackpool version of the 6.75 Litre Crewe V8, which employs a single Garrett turbocharger, without catalysts. Rumor has it that almost all of the Brunei cars were equipped with these special engines that were developed by Cosworth and rated at 530 bhp.

Is it comfortable in there? Who knows. When it looks like that it really doesn't matter. This car demonstrates the full capability of the now defunct Heuliez to design and build to an exacting standard.

Once again, bold colors were selected inside and out. And it works brilliantly.

Note that the windows in the black car are reflective instead of transparent. This is not a window tint film added after the car was built. It is listed as part of the specification of some Buccaneers.

The image above shows a pair of bodies sitting on dimensionally stable steel surface plates, meaning that their measurements were being taken to far less than a millimeter. Precise construction of this nature was something that the pre-war coachbuilders would only have dreamed of.

Bentley Twin Turbo Blackpool Engine
Brunei - Blackpool Project 1997

Price: £5,100.00 (VAT included)

Scroll over the thumbnails to enlarge

Description

Bentley "Blackpool Project" engine

The Blackpool project was a secretive project carried out on behalf of the Sultan of Brunei by Bentley. The project consisted of a series of special engined vehicles to be made for the Sultan with engines producing significantly more power than the standard fit engines. Along with the special vehicles, spare engines were made for each of the vehicles and it is one of these spare engines that we have available from the Blackpool Project. The engine is all new (Bench run and tested).

The Project was a joint venture between Bentley and Cosworth engine developers. It consisted of taking the standard single turbo 6.75 ltr. V 8 Aluminium alloy engine and refining it further with the fitting of twin turbos and twin liquid cooled charge coolers as per the current Arnage T twin turbo engines. The Blackpool engines were developed to produce 530 HP and one we have dyno tested produced over 1000 Nm torque of 730 lb/ft. Tested by Owen Developments in our own Racing Bentley Turbo R.

The engines are complete with all ancillaries (starter motors, water pumps, alternators, turbos, charge coolers, water pipes and hoses, air induction pipes and hoses, fuel lines etc.) engine wiring harnesses. The base core of the engine is a 1997 Bentley Turbo engine significantly and further refined by Cosworth to include polishing, balancing and porting, new inlet manifolds and charge coolers etc. These engines can be used as a doner core (Short engine) for standard 1997 - 2003 single turbo set-ups or as complete units for special projects. The standard Bentley gearbox GM 4L80E is included with this engine and is also new.

Several of the Blackpool engines have come up for sale over the years and many remain tucked away in various storage facilities. Phantom Motor Cars, Ltd. of Surrey England, presented this one, mated to a gearbox, for sale in the early 2000s for a reasonable £ 5100.

BENTLEY CONTINENTAL R FOUR-DOOR AND LIMOUSINE

Project P140 was a four-door Continental R, of which 19 examples were made. Styling was carried out by Hawtal Whiting's Goeff Matthews and Jonathan Gould, under the direction of Crewe's Graham Hull. The chassis numbers are:

- SCBZH04A1SCH00221
- SCBZH04A3SCH00222
- SCBZH04ASSCH00223
- SCBZH04A7SCH00224
- SCBZH04A9SCH00225
- SCBZH04AOSCH00226
- SCBZH04A6SCH00227
- SCBZH04A8SCH00228
- SCBZH04AXSCH00229
- SCBZH04A6SCH00230
- SCBZH04A8SCH00231
- SCBZH04AXSCH00232
- SCBZH04A1SCH00233
- SCBZH04A3SCH00234
- SCBZH04ASSCH00235
- SCBZH04A7SCH00236
- SCBZH04A9SCH00237
- SCBZH04A0SCH00238
- SCBZH04A2SCH00239

Project P144 was the Continental R LWB. There was also an offshoot called P144A, which was the armored variant. The engine is the Bentley Continental R Sufacon engine, without catalyst.

The LWB cars are four inches longer than the standard car. A total of twenty cars were made. Twelve of the normal LWB variant and an additional eight armored examples.

- SCBZH04A3SCH00251
- SCBZH04A5SCH00252
- SCBZH04A7SCH00253
- SCBZH04A9SCH00254
- SCBZH04A0SCH00255
- SCBZH04A2SCH00256
- SCBZH04A4SCH00257
- SCBZH04A6SCH00258
- SCBZH04A8SCH00259
- SCBZH04A4SCH00260
- SCBZH04A6SCH00261
- SCBZH04A8SCH00262
- SCBZH04AXSCH00263
- SCBZH04A1SCH00264
- SCBZH04A9SCH00271
- SCBZH04A0SCH00272
- SCBZH04A2SCH00273
- SCBZH04A4SCH00274
- SCBZH04A6SCH00275
- SCBZH04A8SCH00276

The example below is listed in the records as being a LWB variant and is armor plated. Note the bonnet vents.

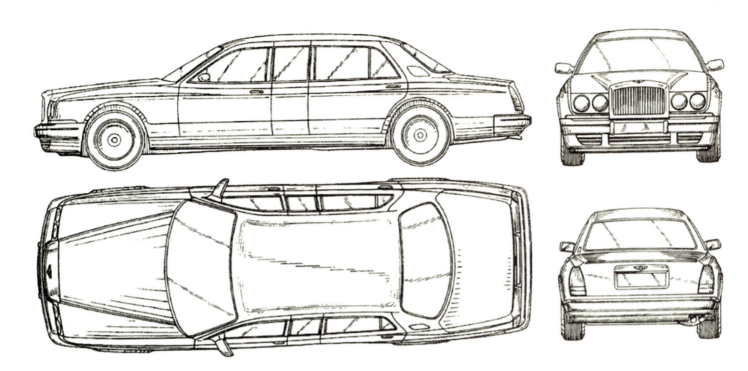

Two of these fabulous looking limousines were made in 1995. The engine is the same unit that is in The Bentley Continental R "Sufacon". One car was Black and the other one was Royal blue. The interior colors were also Black and Royal blue. The blue one is still seen in use quite frequently in the UK.

The chassis numbers for the two Continental R Limousines are:

- SCBZH00A6SCH00041
- SCBZH00A8SCH00042

CONTINENTAL R SPORTS ESTATE

The Bentley Continental R Sports Estate is arguably the most well-resolved of all of the Brunei designs. It looks fabulous from every angle; as if this body configuration had been part of the plan from the beginning. As you can see from the official company brochures, it was available with "protection," which means armor-plating. Of course, if you need that sort of protection, driving around in an attention-getting bespoke Bentley instead of a generic grey mid-size sedan might not be the best of ideas, but practicality rarely comes into play when we are talking about Bentleys. One of the more interesting aspects of the various Continental R Sports Estates seen on these pages is the wide variety of wheel designs that were fitted to them. Some of them impact the overall look of the car more than others. It is also rather peculiar that the car in the image below was allowed to be used in a brochure without its lug nut covers.

Project P130 was the Continental R Estate. 16 cars were made between 1993 and 1994 including a few armored examples known as P130A. They were styled by Simon Loasby and Hawtal Whiting in the UK.

Model year 1993 chassis numbers:

- SCBZH04D8PCH00201
- SCBZH04DXPCH00202
- SCBZH04D3PCH00204
- SCBZH04D5PCH00205
- SCBZH04D7PCH00206
- SCBZH04D9PCH00207

Model year 1995 chassis numbers:

- SCBZH04A2SCH00208
- SCBZH04A4SCH00209
- SCBZH04A0SCH00210
- SCBZH04A2SCH00211
- SCBZH04A4SCH00212
- SCBZH04A6SCH00213
- SCBZH04A8SCH00214
- SCBZH04AXSCH00215
- SCBZH04A1SCH00216
- SCBZH04C1SCH00217

Confirmation Of Order

Ordered by	
Date of Order	21/5/97
Confirmed by	
Date of confirmation	26/5/97
Quantity ordered	4
Anticipated delivery	3 - 3rd Quarter 1998
	1 - 4th Quarter 1998
Price agreed	£1.10m each
Payment terms	40% upon order
	30% January 1998
	15% April 1998
	15% upon delivery

ORIGINAL RENDERING OF SPORTS ESTATE

These two images are from what must be among the most sought-after, but never found Rolls-Royce and Bentley brochures; the one for the Protected Continental R Sports Estate, the armored variant of the Continental R Sports Estate.

The elegance of the Continental R Sports Estate is striking. One wonders if this body style could have found mass market success, especially in Europe where station wagons continued to be popular throughout the 1990s.

The interior details differ somewhat from the normal Continental R, particularly in the door trim.

Photo: Basman007

BENTLEY CONTINENTAL R SUPER SHORT AND SWB

Project P115 was a version of the Continental R. It was four inches shorter than the standard car. Of course, the Blackpool engine was the power source. One car was made.

The chassis number was SCB-ZH04C9RCH00413

In the 1996 model year, another version of the Super Short was developed under project code P117. It is unclear exactly how it differed from P115, but company documents note that P117 was what became the Continental T that was available to the public.

BENTLEY DOMINATOR

The Bentley Bentayga dominates the enthusiast magazine headlines these days and is billed as Bentley's first SUV. That isn't true at all. Bentley's first SUV was the Dominator, of which at least six were made for the Brunei royals in 1995 or 1996. They were built using a third generation Range Rover chassis and running gear, mated to the famous Crewe 6 ¾L engine. It has been said that when the Bentayga was being developed, one of these was borrowed to have as a reference point for the design team.

It remains to be seen if that is true. Little is actually known about them. We are fortunate that once again, quick-thinking airport-working car enthusiasts were able to snap pictures as they were being transported.

Interestingly, this Dominator is finished in the same interior and exterior color combination as the Turbo R Val d'Isere estate shown earlier. A number of Bentley B3s were finished in this livery as well.

If you look carefully, you can see that the tail gate has a split design, meaning that the glass and its metal surround opens upward and the lower portion opens downward.

BENTLEY GRAND PRIX 190

Known as project P250, the Bentley Grand Prix was a high performance, 190 mph supercar with four-wheel drive and an aluminum body.

It was styled by Design Research Associates in the UK and engineered by the now-defunct Hawtal Whiting in both the suburban Detroit office and in the UK.

Six were made:

- SCBZH04C4RCH00361
- SCBZH04C7RCH00362
- SCBZH04C9RCH00363
- SCBZH04CORCH00364
- SCBZH04C2RCH00365
- SCBZH04C4RCH00366

Seen here is the Grand Prix undergoing high speed testing on the MIRA track in the UK

BENTLEY GRAND TOURER IMPERIAL

Very little is known about Project P270, the Bentley Grand Tourer Imperial, other than the fact that six were made with the following chassis numbers;

- SCBZH04C2SCH00341
- SCBZH04C4SCH00342
- SCBZH04C6SCH00343
- SCBZH04C8SCH00344
- SCBZH04A1SCH00345
- SCBZH04A1SCH00346

BENTLEY GRAND TOURER MONTE CARLO

Six examples were made of the Bentley Monte Carlo, project P260. In some company documents, it is referred to as the Bentley Grand Tourer Monte Carlo. It is Continental R-based and has a removeable hard roof.

The six cars carried the following chassis numbers;
- SCBZH04C7SCH00321
- SCBZH04C0SCH00323
- SCBZH04C4SCH00325
- SCBZH04C9SCH00322
- SCBZH04C2SCH00324
- SCBZH04C6SCH00326

BENTLEY HIGHLANDER

Of all of the Brunei cars, the Rapier is the one that has had the most public exposure. For a period, it was often seen parked in front of various high end London shops and in front of various English homes, almost always with a driver inside, waiting patiently.

It's also the Brunei car that bucks Rolls-Royce and Bentley styling conventions the most. Nothing about it says "Crewe" very loudly, but there are a few telltale cues such as the wheels and a few chrome bits, which look very Bentley. For students of car design, this model falls squarely in the middle of the "jelly bean" look that was all the rage in the late 1980s through the mid-1990s. There were plenty of mainstream cars from this era that have now been forgotten, but that also come from this school of styling. Examples of the jelly bean look from around the would be the second generation Ford Scorpio from Europe, the Ford Taurus in America, and the Mazda 929 in Japan.

This car happens to have been designed and engineered in the USA at Irvine, California's Aria-Group, a firm widely respected within the industry for prototype development.

The wonderful design theme sketch above was what guided the actual development of the car through the digital surfacing stage and the clay model stage. It's a rare treat to be able to see a sketch from such a secretive project.

An early proposal for the interior of the Highlander can be seen in these CAD images.

At first glance, the five images here look like photographs, but it is easy to see that they are actually digital images of a finished car in various settings. Keep in mind that these digital renderings were created in the mid-1990s. They represented the highest state-of-the-art in terms of digital visualization technology. Readers from Southern California may recognize some of the scenes as being prominent offices and restaurants around Irvine and Newport Beach. These images were created to show the customer exactly what the finished cars would look like in the real world, in different lighting situations and from different views.

They were quiet successful. Note that the real cars photographed on the street look no different from these images created before they existed.

Even the Brunei royals occasionally need to run to the shops, where intrepid enthusiasts can snap pictures of their cars.

Project P560 was a request for the delivery of six cars to eventually be named Highlander. They were the very first Crewe products to have benefitted from 3D visualization tools. They were an evolution of Project P255, the Rapier, and for many years, enthusiasts have believed this car to be called Rapier. The project began in August 1995 and was styled by Charles Tayler of DZN Design, of Irvine, California. The company was later renamed Aria-Group. It was constructed by Metalcrafters, also of the Los Angeles area.

Chief Engineer was Clive Hawkins, who is more recently known as the man behind the Aria FXE supercar. The chassis numbers are:

- SCBZH16C7TCH00428
- SCBZH16C7TCH00429
- SCBZH16C6TCH00430
- SCBZH16C8TCH00431
- SCBZH16CXTCH00432
- SCBZH16C1TCH00433

Even the wheel design for Rapier was of a bespoke design.

BENTLEY JAVA

Rolls-Royce had a second, less expensive model-line under consideration in the late 1980s and into the 1990s. The project was deemed to be most appropriate for the Bentley brand and the prototype was unveiled at the Geneva Motor Show in March 1994 and was displayed strictly as a concept car. Although the project died on the vine as a production car, The Sultan of Brunei liked it enough to commission a batch of copies which included coupés, convertibles, and wagons. It is said that they are powered by a BMW 4-litre V8 with twin turbochargers and an intercooler and were tuned by Alpina in Germany. The Javas were constructed in model years 1994, 1995, and 1996.

The green Java concept car above was shown to qualified clients at a private reception at the famous Pebble Beach Concours d'Elegance. The interior differs slightly from that of the Brunei Javas.

Transporting the cars by air meant that they would be vulnerable to photography by car enthusiast employees of the airport who were lucky enough to see them.

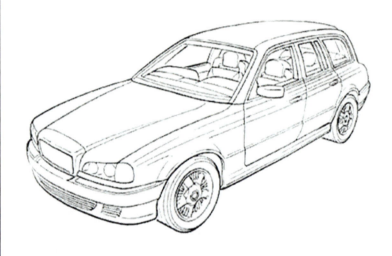

Java Estate

Technical Handbook

Produced for   The exclusive use of the motor vehicle technicians serving the Royal Family of Brunei

Vehicle Identification Numbers   From •SCBVH99C5TCH 00492•

TSD 6087   March 1998

Naturally, Crewe produced service manuals for each of the bespoke models commissioned by the Brunei royals. The cover to the left illustrates the Java Estate.

The chassis numbers of 12 of the 18 cars are known:

- *SCBVH99C8RCH00480*
- *SCBVH99CXRCH00481*
- *SCBVH99D2RCH00483*
- *SCBVH99C1RCH00482*
- *SCBVH99C5RCH00484*
- *SCBVH99C7RCH00485*
- *SCBVH99C5TCH00492*
- *SCBVH99C7TCH00493*
- *SCBVH99C2TCH00496*
- *SCBVH99C9TCH00494*
- *SCBVH99C0TCH00495*
- *SCBVH99C4TCH00497*

The Java, designed internally at the Rolls-Royce studio, was constructed on a BMW 5-Series platform and used a BMW 3.5 litre V8 intercooled twin turbo engine mated to a four-speed automatic gearbox. It was said to be able to produce zero-to-sixty times of 5.6 seconds and had a top speed in excess of 170 mph. These were extraordinary numbers at that time. The coupe was Project P700. The convertible was Project P705. The wagon was Project P710.

BENTLEY PEGASUS

Project P650 was the Bentley Pegasus Coupe, P655 was the convertible, and P660 was the wagon.

Very little is known about the Bentley Pegasus except that 18 were made. Six were coupes, six were sedans, and six were wagons. They are based on the widened Continental R platform.

Nine of the 18 chassis numbers are known:

- SCBZH16C9TCH00440
- SCBZH16C0TCH00441
- SCBZH16C4TCH00443
- SCBZH16CXTCH00446
- SCBZH16C1TCH00447
- SCBZH16C3TCH00448
- SCBZH16CSTCH00449
- SCBZH16CSTCH00452
- SCBZH16C7TCH00453

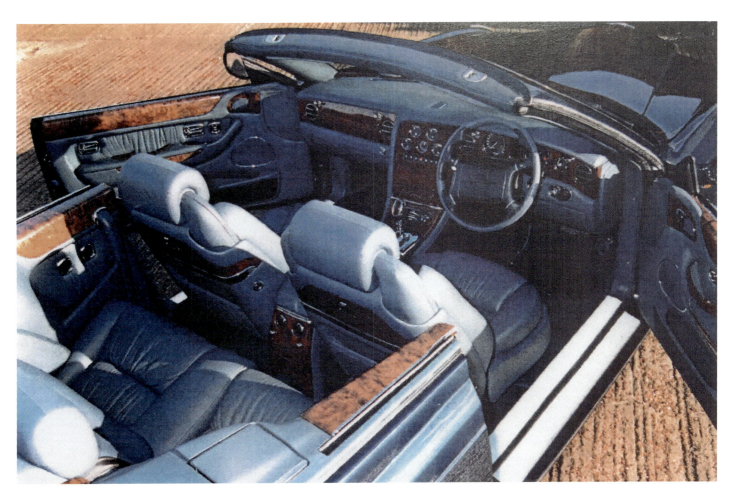

ROLLS-ROYCE PHANTOM MAJESTIC

Ironically, one of the most mysterious of the Brunei cars is one of the ones that enthusiasts would most like to know about and to see good pictures of, inside and out. These images, regardless of their poor quality, show us that what we have on our hands with this car is what every Rolls-Royce fan has dreamed of; a modern incarnation of the Phantom V styling, with modern mechanicals.

We know that four copies of Project P210 were made, all constructed in 1995. The cars feature the 6 ¾ L Rolls-Royce V8 engine with urbocharging, as used in the 1995 Rolls-Royce Flying Spur, but without catalytic converters. They are right hand drive and are equipped with airbags. They were built by the French coachbuilder Heuliez, to the very highest standard, but it is unclear if they were also designed by Heuliez.

The chassis numbers are;

- SCAZH04A2SCH00021
- SCAZH04A4SCH00022
- SCAZH04A6SCH00023
- SCAZH04A8SCH00024

It appears to be fabulous in every way. We can only hope that better pictures will eventually emerge.

The quality of the construction is evident in this image of the "body in white" on a dimensionally stable surface plate inside of the Heuliez works. Clearly, this car is as thoroughly engineered as any regular production car.

Looking at the picture below, it is clear that not only has this car been engineered to a high standard, but that it has been constructed completely out of metal. There are no structural plastic substrates anywhere in sight, which is not the case in any modern car; not even in production Rolls-Royce motorcars from this era.

ROLLS-ROYCE PHANTOM ROYALE

It is believed that this rather striking motorcar is called the Rolls-Royce Royale. Six examples were built by Italy's legendary design house and coachbuilder, Bertone. These images appeared in a Bertone corporate brochure that was printed near the end of Bertone's financial unwinding. The brochures provided no additional or useful information about the cars. The cars were built on the same special ZH chassis that so many of the other Brunei cars used. Both cars used a version of the Rolls-Royce 6 ¾ L engine with a single Garrett turbocharger, a cross-bolted crankshaft, and without catalytic converters. They are right hand drive cars and they employ those pesky active seat belts that US spec short wheelbase cars had from 1987-1989. The cars were built concurrently and have sequential chassis numbers.

Just as you would expect, every inch appeared strikingly well-finished when viewed from any angle.

Six copies of the Rolls-Royce Phantom Royale were built between 1995 and 1997. Company documents refer to it as both the Phantom Royale and Phantom VII Royale. Internally known as Project P200, this seven-seat limousine is based on a stretched and widened Continental R platform. Early cars used the drivetrain of the 1995 Rolls-Royce Flying Spur. The later cars made in 1997 use the mechanicals of the 1997 Turbo R, which was essentially the same as the Flying Spur drivetrain, but with some small detail changes. There are four known chassis numbers and two that remain a mystery.

Model year 1995

- SCAZW04A8SCH80138
- SCAZH04A3SCH00013
- SCAZH04C35CH00014

Model year 1997

- SCAZH16C4VCH00465

ROLLS-ROYCE PHANTOM V

Project P290 was a modern Phantom V limousine. Although it appears to be a Phantom V from the late 1960s, it employed a normally aspirated Silver Spur drivetrain and associated mechanicals. There were many other modern elements as well. For example, the wheels were milled from billet aluminum to look like traditional steel wheels with hub caps. It is said that in 2000 it was returned to Crewe to be fitted with an Arnage engine. The chassis number is SCAZH00D6SCH00071.

BENTLEY PHOENIX

The Bentley Phoenix, Project P105, was another version of the Continental R convertible. It featured the Brunei-exclusive Sufacon engine, without catalyst. Some of the cars were fitted with louder exhaust systems and some received reflective glass. The chosen color schemes were Masons Black with Black hides, Sapphire Blue with Royal Blue hides, Tudor Red with St James Red hides, and Titanium with Slate hides. Nine cars were produced.

All nine chassis numbers are known.

Model year 1995

- SCBZH04A7SCH00141
- SCBZH04A9SCH00142
- SCBZH04AOSCH00143
- SCBZH04A2SCH00144
- SCBZH04A4SCH00145
- SCBZH04A6SCH00146

Model year 1996

- SCBZH04C6TCH00173
- SCBZH04C8TCH00174
- SCBZH04CXTCH00175

BENTLEY RAPIER

Rapier, Project P255, is the Java project fitted with the 6 ¾L Rolls-Royce engine instead of the BMW 4.4L. The major visual difference is in the interior, which is much more driver-oriented than Java.

ROLLS-ROYCE SILVER CLOUDESQUE

We know that four copies of the Silver Cloud Limousine were produced. Confusingly, company documents refer to the cars as both the Cloudesque and the Silver Cloud Limousine. The project name was P240. The first two cars were ordered in 1995 in something called "Special Grey" and the two built in 1997 were simply called black.

The cars were built on the SZ Mulliner Park Ward Touring Limousine chassis and were styled by Futura Design in the UK. It is certainly one of the more intriguing designs for Brunei. Two cars went to Brunei and at least one remains in the UK. The UK car is registered N282 and the Brunei cars bear the number plates BQ 6363 and KF 7899. That is the full extent of the information that is known to the enthusiast world about this most wonderous of things, the Rolls-Royce Cloudesque.

In this image of the interior, the Silver Spur origins are clear.

Three chassis numbers are known:

Model year 1995

- SCAZH000SSCH00060
- SCAZH00A8SCH00062

Model year 1997

- SCAZH13C4VCH00468

BENTLEY SILVERSTONE

The Bentley Silverstone was another Brunei car that was designed and constructed in the USA. This time, the coachbuilder was ASC, once known as American Sunroof Corporation and later known as American Specialty Cars. Today the company is simply known as ASC and is still involved in the automotive design business. Within the industry it was well-known for being a quality builder and produced a number of popular mainstream models such as the cabriolet variant of the Porsche 944 S2, the convertible versions of Nissan's 240SX and 300ZX, Mitsubishi's 3000GT Spyder retractable hardtop, and the Toyota Solara, among many others.

The designer of the Silverstone was Douglas Ungemach, a seasoned designer who flies under the radar, but has laid his pen to many production car design projects. The car was developed and built in ASC's California studios.

Project P150 was a retractable hardtop convertible, styled by Doug Ungemach at ASC in Detroit, Michigan, USA. It was constructed by Metalcrafters of Los Angeles, California. Eight examples were made between 1994 and 1995.

Seven of the eight chassis number are known:

- SCBZH04A0RCH00301
- SCBZH04A2RCH00302
- SCBZH04A4RCH00303
- SCBZH04A6RCH00304
- SCBZH04AXRCH00306
- SCBZH04C3SCH00476
- SCBZH04CSSCH00477

In this collection of rare pictures you can see just how well resolved the design of the Silverstone was. Beyond that, it is clear that the interior was as well-executed and refined as any production Bentley.

BENTLEY SPECTRE

Project P104 was the Bentley Spectre; which, like the Phoenix, was based on the Continental R and was developed at the same time as what was to become the mainstream Bentley Azure. Nine copies were built. The Spectre and its sister car, the Phoenix, were the first Crewe cars to use electronics traction control, which was necessitated by the incredible power of the Sufacon engine. Spectre used wider diameter wheels than the standard Bentley Azure to try to cope with the additional power.

Other than the seat styling, there is no clear difference between this and the production Azure.

ROLLS-ROYCE STATESMAN

Two copies of the Rolls-Royce Statesman, Project P450, were made. It seems to share the styling of the Rolls-Royce Phantom Majestic. It appears that the major difference is the body construction. The Statesman seems to have employed conventional construction techniques, whereas the Phantom Majestic was chemically bonded. The chassis numbers are unknown.